Socialism and Capitalism…

Let's change that to:

Government Controlled Market and

Free Market

C. James Green

absolutevyl

publishing

i

2017 by C. James Green

ISBN-13:
978-1720869139

ISBN-10:
1720869138

Contents

Preface

This book serves as an activity book for beginning economics students that I have taught for several years. It is not overly academic as the students generally have to find and fill in the quotes themselves then describe as best they can the difference between government controlled markets and free markets. Socialism, social welfare as well as politics and administration all go into our daily decisions. The lack of knowledge on the subject of Socialism/Communism and Capitalism in today's society, especially academia is quite astounding and I hope the readers of this book can better understand the definitions of the words and the consequences of that ignorance. This book is meant to start a dialog into the realities Socialism and Socialist countries and leaders have purported onto mankind

Introduction

Quotes and the parameters of knowledge.

We know that certain systems do not work. Theocracy or rule by religion does not accept outside opinion and creates a large swath of inequality. To say a leader is given orders by God, means he or she has the innate capability of corruption. As some whom say they have been touched by God could in fact be false prophets. These people could use the force of the unknown to their advantage and harm others who do not believe. Also, Monarchy or rule by family is also a failed system. Much like religious rule, the family is concerned only with itself and as we have seen in many cases in the past the family tends to purge (kill) outsiders in order to maintain its rule. That leaves us with only three other types of political systems, Socialism/Communism, Democracy and Republic.

Socialism/Communism lends itself to a similar system as Theocracy and Monarchy. Religion is replaced by the state. The state is its own tenucratic system of power elites with all power lying in the hands of one party. These elites then make rules and laws for the masses to obey that they believe is best for them. The people have no real say and in the end the pre-planned state apparatus controls every aspect from outputs of production to what and when the citizenry can buy. Leading us into total Democracy. Which when all decisions are left up to the masses to vote upon, will ultimately be voted into by the majority leaving the minority to fend for themselves and left out of the political process. However despite its flaws Democratic countries do enjoy one thing the others lack, that of a decreased amount of conflict with each other. Lastly there is the Constitutional Republic which is based upon law and allows for minority rights (as seen in the United States), though a flawed system but it does enjoy personal freedoms some of the others do not (There are many others but we do not have the time to explore them for this enquiry).

Unfortunately this book is not so much a political book but one of terminology. Here we will delve into the terms Socialism/Communism and Capitalism by looking at quotes from various people. Beyond the terms themselves there is what will be called a "mystery" to one term and a definitive of the other. Socialism (or communism) seems to leave the ignorant to pontificate as to what it is. This mystery of Socialism has made people since its inception see it as a good thing, something repairable, something divine, something uber-human, an ideal state to be achieved by mankind and mankind's answer to all its evil and wickedness. Capitalism is seen as mankind's wickedness and its goals of selfish intent of accumulation of capital above all is the greatest of man's sin.

Herein we can leave discourse and start the dialog about the terms Socialism and Capitalism. The way this book does this is to change the terms into what they are and let people understand exactly what they are; Socialism is a Government Controlled Market and Capitalism is the Free Market. From here on in these two terms will be used to define how we see the world and clarify the ideal state for these ever faithful Government Controlled Market believers.

Government Controlled Markets (Socialism/Communism) is latent. When the system we know of as Socialism is implemented fully it is done by simply controlling of markets by the government. Does anyone fully trust governments without a shred of doubt that they are benevolent? No. Governments are not to be trusted and should be contained. Every person wants to be left alone with little to no interference in their lives. So Government Controlled Markets are inherently bad. When the government controls inputs and controls what and how we choose to live, it never ends in success. It is now 2018, and every country that has attempted to have a Government Controlled Market system has either become a failed state (USSR, the East Bloc, Venezuela etc.) or has killed, murdered and suppressed its people (Cuba, North Korea). Why do some still cling to the mystery of the ideal state? Why is it taught as an ideal? We already know the consequences and they are all terrible.

To the opposite end of the spectrum the evil Free Market (Capitalism) also remains. When does the word free equate evil? Free markets are just that, free. We can choose to buy, work, live and do what we want. The Free Market may have some losers, but even if you lose, you still have a chance to try again. The Free Market may not be fair, but yet it is fair in that you do have a choice. Free Markets allow for innovation and the ability to improve one's situation through creative means. Therein if the word is changed to Free Market as opposed to Capitalism, we know it is much friendlier and cannot be questioned as to what it is.

Government Controlled Market or Free Market, which would you choose?

The rest of the book is sectioned into three parts; the first chapter looks at quotes with the word Socialism in them, the second chapter looks at quotes with both Socialism and Capitalism within them and the third chapter with quotes that only have Capitalism in them. After each quote there is a short dialog into each quote and a short attempt to dissect each quote and provide meaning. The purpose of the book is to challenge the reader to think, to argue and know more about the terms and the words surrounding them and their systems. To build a more just society we should all be able to look at words and the meanings behind them, rather than just listening to catchphrases and soundbites by famous people. Look at the words, what is their intent and why are they being used in this light. There are many quotes using these words. I have limited this book to less than 10 quotes per section but hopefully the reader can find the exercise meaningful and worthwhile in the quest for knowledge.

Chapter I.

Socialism Quotes

1.

"All Government Controlled Markets involve slavery."

Here is a classic line about socialism. When one is taught about socialism in school, it is always about being fair and balanced but does not reveal the actuality, that of the state and its control. Much like slavery as the author points out, everyone gets some form of housing, food, and healthcare and as Lebowitz (2010) points out, pure freedom. In his book the socialist alternative he says, "Marx had a vision of an alternative-the society of associated producers 'a society of free individuality, based on the universal development of individuals and on their subordination of their communal, social productivity as their social wealth' guides society" (pg. 21, Lebowitz, 2010).

What distinguishes Marx's vision of the freedom of individuality more than the chains of society other than being linked and bound by chains? Anyone can do this at any time. Commit a crime, go to jail, and receive everything free from the state. Give up everything you have to become a Socialist and allow the state to run everything for you. Government Controlled market economies lock each and every person into a small box, a spoke in the wheel, a voiceless thimble on the finger of society that must accept what is given to him or her, to be used by the state and eventually thrown aside when they are no longer useful.

2.

"Like the Phoenix, Government Controlled
Markets are reborn from every pile of
ashes left day in, day out, by burnt-out
human dreams and charred hopes."

This quote spells out the "ideal" world hard-edge socialists believe the failures and disturbing irrelevancies of actual socialism can be changed into something true and relevant. Communist wanna-be's and Socialist dreamers will always say that what has occurred in the past, can be improved upon and a new form of socialism will be better and make the perfect society. These uninformed people do not see Government Controlled Markets as any type of sin, these believers cannot see the final corruption that will take place when the government does actually have control of every aspect of the market. These idealists can read the works of Marx and see the revolution, but do not see the other stages of government controlled development that will eventually ensue, as author X says "There are three confirmed roads to development in socialist countries, 1. Revolution, 2. Normalization, and 3. Militarization." (Kornai, 1992).

All roads to Communism must go through some form of revolution, be it a bloody revolution as in Russia and Cuba, or a social revolution as in Venezuela or Yugoslavia. Though mostly violent, the revolution subsides and the redistribution of wealth takes place and government is formed on this basis in the normalization stage, this is the beginning of eradicating and extermination of old ideas and weeding out of those that are not part of the new guard. Finally there is always militarization. The country becomes a militaristic state, the military is empowered, the people lose all ability to go against the government, if so, and they can be eliminated or sent to jail. All forms of resistance are squashed. Once this happens, total government control of production occurs and pure bureaucracy ensues. Waiting for the real Marxism to show its ugly head again and again, through death and destruction, the perfect system will always be sought by the noble uninformed idiot and history will repeat itself once again.

3.

"In fact, what were called Government Controlled Market countries in Eastern Europe were the most anti-government controlled market systems in the world. Workers had more rights in the United States and England than they had in Russia, and it was somehow still called a Government Controlled Market."

Classic tomfoolery and mincing of words by a well worded writer. By attempting to purvey that these countries were not living the socialist utopia because the workers were so free in capitalist countries actually makes the system look like free marketers see it and how it actually is, a blind spot no one could see. In the first sentence the author negates himself or the utopian countries then compares them to their counterpart, which when people are in a free market society, actually do have more rights as they are free to choose their jobs and are not simply slaves, as we see in governmentally controlled market systems. Workers have freedom to choose their job, to leave their current residence or to stay and possibly change their current conditions. The authors sleight of hand to purvey the notion that a government controlled market country should be the answer falls flat when the language is stripped down to its actual core function.

4.

"Democracy and Government Controlled Markets have nothing in common but one word equality.

But notice the difference: while Democracy seeks equality in liberty, government controlled markets seek equality in restrained servitude."

This classic quote resonates the slavery quote from quote number one. One must give up ones liberty and freedom and this is done by pure servitude, which is restrained – not willingly- given up as government controlled markets are a sort of slave like inhibited manor.

When you concede your individual liberty to the group, you actually lose your liberty. Giving up liberty to the state means giving up everything to the state. If you allow government controlled markets to control your liberty the only thing you will get if you attempt to rebel is jail or death. In government controlled market societies there is no change of hands in the power circle, the party rules everything and the party rules you.

5.

"Yes, in Government Controlled Markets the rich will be poorer but the poor will be poorer. People will lose interest in really working hard and creating jobs."

The quote handles two subjects, poverty and incentives. The first that people under government control will become poorer involves the lack of adequate jobs, especially in times of economic shock, environmental disaster and war. In all three cases the government controlled market economy is unprepared, for example the current state of Venezuela in case number one and North Korea in case number two and the Nazi government in case number three.

Poorness or lack of wealth will come with the lack of incentives. In government controlled market economies workers get paid the same, the only incentive to work then is to look forward to career advancement (tenure). Government controlled countries do not incentivize advancement to all, only those with high test scores or tenure. With the former only a select few can advance, giving less incentive to study for an exam as you can surmise, for example when a test is restricted to the top 4% then only they will advance and the other 96% of the remaining test takers will remain locked within the same position. This leads to the latter case of tenure. Workers will assume that time will give them their advancement without incentive to try hard as pay will always remain the same and advancement will take years, again leading to disincentivization of hard work. When everyone is the same and will be the same for long periods of time with no incentive to advance, life is pointless, work is pointless and much like the pessimist, almost everyone will give up trying for anything in life. Government controlled market societies are suicide.

6.

"Compassion is not weakness, and concern for the unfortunate is not (a) Government Controlled Market."

When an individual sees a stray dog and the dogs big eyes and hunger in its belly the individual will take the dog in, care for it, feed it, give it love and raise it as their own. Each individual takes responsibility to take care of their dogs as they see fit and this compassion for other living beings is our human ability as individuals. Compassion for stray dogs does not make you weak.

A Government entity does not have compassion. When the government controls the market for dogs, the stray dog is gathered up with other stray dogs and all are treated the same. They are all put in an area called the "humane shelter" where they are fed, caged, cleaned well and held for a short time. If the dog is not adopted (often within a week or so) it is euthanized (put to sleep or killed) because the state itself has no concern for the longevity of a dog, for the most part humans too. When government controlled markets rule the state, the individual is disconcerting, individuals are worthless, the group is more important. Therein compassion, care and concern for one another or fellow man is meaningless. If you are deeded worthless, like the stray dog, you will be executed in a government controlled society.

7.

"Government Controlled Markets are the ideal state, but it can never be achieved while man is so selfish."

The author points out that of the ideal state Government Controlled Market society, which can only be done if man releases hisself of his selfish desires. The free market in this case is man's selfish desire to get everything for himself in other words the free market itself is selfish while the Government controlled market is unselfish.

Man's desire for self-preservation is selfish, man's desire for a better life is selfish, and therein the free market is selfish. However to say the government controlled market is unselfish is not possible. Every organization has the same desire. Its very existence. A government controlled society will do everything in its power to remain viable. Even when it fails it will still find a way to remain afloat, even if that means starving, jailing and killing its own people for its ideals. Therefore government controlled market systems are the worst kind of selfish, they are governmentally controlled self-preserving machines without morals or ethics.

8.

"Government Controlled Market is a philosophy of failure, the creed of ignorance, and the gospel of envy, its inherent virtue is the equal sharing of misery."

Envy and misery the two major tenants of the revolution and the militarization factions that evolve in government controlled market economies. Each socialist/communist movement begins with revolution. The revolution is to overthrow the dreaded bourgeoisie, or upper class. In this action we can see the envy of the socialist mind, to make those with more, to give up everything, to take it from them and distribute it back to everyone else (themselves included). However, the revolutionary government controlled marketer does not look at the long run, or even at the past failures of socialism/communism throughout history, instead believe they can improve on its previous failures for their perfect equal societal ideal.

As the past has shown, time and time again, the ideal world lands the government with no choice as to militarize all of society, create order, remove independent thought, making each person a cog in the wheel and the people policed while making moves to engulf other societies and countries under their government control as the socialist mind will see outsiders as something to subdue. The miserable life they lead must be pushed unto others and pushed as an ideal all in the namesake of creating a better human and ideal human society.

9.

"The problem with Government Controlled Markets is that you eventually run out of other people's money."

A key factor of socialism is redistribution of wealth making everyone equal. As the author of this quote points out government does not create money (wealth). Government cannot create wealth, therefore government controlled market economies must constantly be borrowing or taking from others to the point the government controlled market runs out of everything.

Governments cannot predict the weather, natural disasters, societal behaviors or the market and when they do they are more often than not, wrong. Attempting to keep the market on an even trajectory, feed the people or perform simple tasks equal at all times puts governments in a tough predicament, maintaining this equality of outcome. As inpredictability ensues – often for the worse – governments have two options, borrow or plunder. Debt has its own problems which put governments in a constant cycle of repayment – which often ends up in borrowing more to pay off the previous debt. Governments also have the option of plundering – e.g. attack or annex another country. War (plunder) creates nothing and the spoils of war soon get used up and government must plunder again to keep up its citizen's equality. Annexation engulfs the new area into the current areas sphere of influence and in time whatever gains initially incurred from the annexation eventually become morphed into the society as a whole and the cycle repeats itself as the government runs out of resources attempting to maintain every person's equality.

10.

"Government Controlled Markets in general
have a record of failure so blatant that only an
intellectual could ignore or evade it."

The record of failure of every governmentally controlled market economy is, or should be well known worldwide, including academia. However this is almost never the case. In academia almost all subjects somehow teach Marxist theory or teach of socialism as a system of ideal perfection that is always within grasp, but not yet achieved. Socialism is taught as a system of humanity, equal rights, fairness of income and outcome, well-regulated and safe products, free education to all, universal healthcare, equal housing (no homelessness for example), the ability of everyone to achieve their human potential through having the chains of responsibility removed, look towards the future and not the past, once this is achieved everyone will be happy.

In academia the good parts of socialist countries are highlighted and taught while the negative aspects – famine, poor conditions, police control, speech control, threat of death, imprisonment, mass deaths, terrible central planning, inequality amongst the haves in government and the have nots who are not in the government or connected to it, the reliance on the state for everything, and again the constant threat of death and actual death is never discussed. Government intervention in markets is taught as a good, inevitable process and free markets are inherently evil. Academia does not see the reality of the lives of the people only the noble aspects that can be hypothesized, philosophized and romanticized.

Chapter II.

Government Controlled Market and Capitalism Quotes

11.

"We all too often have Government Controlled Markets for the rich and rugged Free Markets for the poor."

Those in power want to remain in power and one way to maintain power is to control the market. This is done through monopoly power and no other force greater than the government can have a monopoly on power.

The government holds the monopoly on what to tax or subsidize, which enterprises to grow and which to discourage. With socialism the government controls these markets creating a power vacuum that is held by those wealthy enough to maintain the market.

Meanwhile the other opportunities that the government markets will not or do not touch are left to the masses to fight over and/or create anew. Survival then becomes the focus of those left out of the monopoly or as we know as government controlled markets.

12.

"I am convinced that the path to a new, better and possible world is not Free Markets, the path is Government Controlled Markets."

To create a better world let the government do it. This quote takes all the responsibility away from the people and places it into the government. Don't worry, don't try, let big brother do it while you rest. Lack of responsibility is a big tool used by the government controllers would like you to imbibe. Responsibility is what humans must deal with on a daily basis – right and wrong, good and bad, expenditure and revenue, profit and loss, cost and benefit, all of which people need to concern when performing any action, that action referred to as, ethics.

However if the government takes responsibility for everything, ethics are not necessary, they are secondary and left up to the state. The lack of individual responsibility can therefore be placed completely on the state and if an individual does something immoral it is the state's fault, the person. A better world according to the author of this quote is to fork over responsibility to the state and therein none of that responsibility lies on you, because you are relieved of its duties.

Therein we can see the government's use of this tool of ease, of a better life within the auspice of government control. No responsibility, you did nothing wrong, blame the system, not yourself. When government controls responsibility, in the end, there is no consequence in its (the government's) actions. The government can therefore commit inhumane acts and that means your individual life is meaningless, you are but a number, a statistic, to be used like a worthless product by the immoral state.

13.

"They talk about the failure of Government Controlled Markets but where is the success of Free Markets in Africa, Asia and Latin America?"

The reference to what Wallerstein (2001) has coined as the periphery of global economies of Africa, Asia and Latin America the author of this quote refers to the inequalities amongst the rich and poor in these areas. To begin with, the free market does contain within it inequality of income amongst people but unlike its counterpart – government controlled markets – the free market has enabled millions in these areas to lift themselves out of extreme poverty.

In 1991 after the fall of the Soviet Union the percent of people living on less than one dollar a day stood at around 47%, then twenty years later that figure dropped to 22%. The OECD showed that Latin Americans living on less than four dollars a day decreased 10% from the year's 2000 to 2010 (Delsol, 2017).

The attempt of the author to use the argument of free market's failures in these areas disregards total global success to attempt to paint the free market as somehow more of a failure than the government controlled market system of socialism, but does elude to socialisms failures but cannot point to any successes of which it has none.

14.

"With the development of industrial Free Markets, a new and unanticipated system of injustice, it is Libertarian Government Controlled Markets that has preserved and extended the radical humanist message of the Enlightenment and the classical liberal ideas that were perverted into an ideology to sustain the emerging social order."

This is a great quote that actually creates a new term, libertarian government controlled markets. There we could leave it simply as an oxymoron, however later in the quote we can see the reference to some kind of ideology. Libertarian government controlled markets is not only proof of double talk but how people are ignorant about the roots of the word socialism. The advent that an ideology is so inset that its pure negation is accepted by the people at large is why we continue to hear about it time and time again.

As people become deeper and deeper ingrained into the thought that government control is the lack of government control (libertarianism) the more they might actually believe in the thought of a true communism or true Marxism as they always believe the epitome of human development. Of course the author attributes a social order to the conception of this term, of which the term social order or social class has its own leanings into Marxism itself. This is the assumption that free markets create social order in the frame of class and class is the government controlled markets true enemy. The true development of humanity is that of classless orderless anarchy ruled by the government, true Marxism.

The attempt to make or create a new society or create a new level of humanity is the goal of government control. This play on words has been tried by the National Socialist Workers Party (Nazi party) in Germany and the Chinese workers party in China. Sustaining social order makes workers go against their own interests in order to bring the entire group down to its lowest performer.

An example of this manipulation is by looking at organizational theorist James Thompson (2003) who visited factories in the 1960's in the US. Thompson was sent to factories to increase workers performance and found that, if in fact a worker was overperforming he was subsequently 'thumped' to slow his performance so as to not outperform his counterparts. The author of this quote is trying to 'thump' the reader by attempting to fool them. Government control works the very same way, make everyone equal even to the point of humiliation.

15.

"During the New Deal people thought to be liberal was to reject Government Controlled Markets on one extreme and Government Controlled Markets on the other hand and to preserve Free Markets through regulation and a social safety net."

This quote claims that regulation and social safety nets could preserve free markets while rejecting government controlled markets to each extreme (socialism and fascism respectively). To assume that a market is free if it is regulated and given cushion when it fails is a genuine distortion of the word free. Regulation itself is restriction, not freedom. A regulated market makes it to where business is limited and a safety net means there is no risk of failure, both forms are of government control.

A case of regulation and safety nets can be seen in the use of beaches in South Korea, in particular during the summer. During the summer the people can rent an umbrella to sit under, while a barrier is set up in the ocean to stop people from going too deep. There, the government regulates the usable space of the beach and the water, regulating one market, in this case recreation goods. In a free market beach people are free to tan, play volleyball, snorkel, ride jet skis, swim, surf and anything you can put your mind to do in this free and open space. With restrictions placed on beach recreation, entire markets suffer. The volleyball market, the jetski market, the surf market etc. Therein we do not see large scale sales of these kinds of products and the Koreans themselves do not take much interest in the sport of swimming and other water activities.

A safety net is also government control of markets by removing risk, any industry can be penetrated without fear of failure. Again in the case of Korea and individual credit. Each person has approximately 2.3 credit cards each and the individual credit of each person on average is roughly 80% of the GDP (Williamson, 2013). Individuals have been bailed out twice by the government buying up their existing debt from lenders and giving the borrowers a clean slate to do reckless spending behavior again and again. The result is over-consumption, terrible waste and pollution problems along with a culture of new (everything must be new all the time). The culture of new is that everything should be bought new and preservation of anything is not considered part of their culture or bad luck. Therefore inflation has increased on all products, creating a cycle which people need more credit to buy newer more expensive products despite need or ability to repay.

Government overreach in the case of regulation and safety nets is still government control. Moving markets, disrupting behavior and restricting behavior, which otherwise would be an individual's free choice is government control and not the free market at all.

16.

"Where there's Free Markets, there'll be Government Controlled Markets, because there is always a response to injustice."

Injustice toward the individual is exactly what you get from government controlled anything. This quote then is a classic oxymoron where the author has been led to believe the correction of free markets is government interference and in the case of socialism, total government control of markets. Therein the author of this quote thinks that free markets are out of control and injust, that the freedom of choice provided each individual's decision needs to be contained or controlled/ corrected by the state. Begging the question, do individuals need to be controlled by an outside force such as the government? The overbearing state in this case should correct the injustice of a few individuals choice to harm another or choose a specific product that may or may not harm his or herself?

An example of this instance is the case of state controlled oil. In Venezuela, the government seized control of the oil and put the government in charge of production and distribution, creating a socialized state in the process. The reason they gave, that free market trading of oil was unjust to the people of Venezuela who should have total ownership of their natural resources which were being stolen by them from greedy foreign companies. This commodity if left to the free market would not have much impact on the economy of the country as a whole, it would simply be one commodity amongst many. However when the price of oil (a freely traded commodity on world markets (with no control by the Venezuelan government) dropped, so too did the entire country's income, followed by hyperinflation, lack of goods, unemployment (or lack of basic income in the case of socialist governments) has injured the people. If a select few chose to invest in oil and took the loss individually the economy would be only slightly shocked, but the entire country now suffers due to government control.

Free markets may not promise everyone everything they want, but can give them what they need, governmentally controlled markets cannot. People my reap some benefits in the short run, but in the long run everyone suffers, and as a government tries to keep power and maintain its control on the market people suffer and die. In government controlled markets there is no choice, and no alternative, therefore ultimately no justice.

17.

"Feminism is a Government Controlled Market, anti-family, political movement that encourages women to leave their husbands, kill their children, practice witchcraft, destroy Free Markets and become lesbians."

The quote equates the political movement of feminism with communism how communism will usher in a women's utopia, if looked at from a government control perspective, yes it would. The state can be everything for a woman, the provider, the family, the religion and the freedom from children. The goal of Socialism is all of these things as the state creates its own religion around itself and believes it can provide for every person, removing the family and indeed humanity in its process. The author of this quote compares government control to feminism which looks to destroy what they see as a patriarchy and replace it with a matriarchical society.

The oppression of women – as seen in feminism-as with the proletariat in Marxism, the release of free markets means now the government can control the behavior of men making them equal to women. According to feminists government controlled markets will equalize the playing field by taking from the upper class (men) and distributing it equally to everyone else (women), removing men from society and allowing women to live in a women dominated society. Wherein the state can replace men, leaving only women as men are obsolete. The classless society of one type of person, nameless faceless, decisionless is the goal of socialism.

18.

"I was not chosen to be president to restore
Free Markets to (my country): I was selected
to defend, maintain and continue to perfect
the Government Controlled Market, not
destroy it."

The continual perfecting of government controlled markets is the goal of every good Marxist that sees the system as still viable, despite all of socialism/communisms failures. The continual perfecting or the thought of every new Marxist/Socialist/Government Controlled Market economist believes they can achieve, propels them, somehow towards finding that ever evading treasure of the perfect society. Perfecting this ideal society is done for no other purpose than attempting to perfect humanity, mold man after society or society after man.

This quest for perfection is akin to that of a scientist that tries the same formula again and again, only to attain the same result every time, failure. A good scientist would accept failure and move on to another experiment using the failures learned to make the new project succeed, but this is not true with humanity and social theories. Once caught up in their ideal, caught in a lie, they need to build up falsehoods after falsehoods to cover up the previous falsehoods in order not to concede defeat, or get caught in said lie. Socialism has never had a success story. Government controlled market societies must harm their people in order to continue with the lies, denial and deceit it takes to maintain their failed system.

19.

"I was guilty of judging Free Markets by its operations and Government Controlled Markets by its hopes and aspirations; Free Markets by its works and Government Controlled Markets by its literature."

The free market can be easily judged, quantified, broken down and assessed. In the free market an individual or product is judged by its successes and failures. If consumers wish to purchase a product its value increases, if not its value decreases and eventually disappears. This cannot be said of government controlled market products or services as a product or service provided by or subsidized by the government can remain, despite non-profitability, with hopes and aspirations that it will either one day be profitable or retain its value.

Chapter III.

Free Market quotes

20.

"Free Markets are the astounding belief that the most wickedest of men will do the most wickedest of things for the greatest good of everyone."

There is a Korean fable of two brother's one named Heungbu and the other Norbu. Heungbu was the good brother who did as he was told while Norbu was naughty and always tried new things which got him into trouble. Whenever Norbu got into trouble, Heungbu would come to his rescue. In this fable the steady brother was humble lived humbly and did not seek or have much wealth, Norbu on the other hand was always trying new schemes, sometimes successful, sometimes failing.

It is true that some of the best inventions and methods for innovation ae not safe and do contain risk, but without those new inventions or innovations society would not move forward and creates a stagnate market. Safety and security, though very noble attributes can also hinder the economy. Risk and ingenuity, the attempt at trying new methods has made our life easier, not harder for everyone and should be rewarded on the free market.

21.

"There is a contradiction between market liberalism and political liberalism. The market liberals of today want family values, less government and maintain the traditions of society. However, we must face the cultural contradiction of Free Markets. The progress of Free Markets, which necessitates a consumer culture, undermines the values which render Free Markets possible."

Free markets do foster good behaviors as the quote refers to, but also foster bad behaviors which the quote refers to as consumer culture. There are other behaviors that are perhaps worse than consumer culture that may harm society even more, as freedom does allow for each individual to achieve as much or as little as he or she has the ability or drive to achieve.

When bad behavior is looked at as a sin, of all of St. Thomas Aquinas' seven deadly sins, consumer culture can be construed as leading not only to gluttony, but also envy, greed and possibly pride.

Therein lies the virtue of individual responsibility. The freedom to commit these sins also allows for each person his or her own sense of responsibility. Pride in the free market can be connected with honesty, your pride in having a good product will win you more customers. One's anger, greed and envy can also propel the individual to be better than their competitors. One's gluttony will lead to sloth allowing competitors to innovate and get ahead of those that are obsolete or no longer competitive to move aside for better products, which in turn benefits consumers.

The free market is free and therefore ripe for the possibility of sin but also ripe with the possibility for

that sin to propel the market and society to better itself
in the long run.

22.

"We have two evils to fight, Free Markets and racism. We must destroy both racism and Free Markets."

This quote is directly targeted at government market control. Despite the obvious destruction of free markets, the overtones equating race and free markets is also included in the quote. This type of propaganda is so blatant that is shows how the author of the quote does not understand either concept and simply wants to control both aspects of their society. A free market is free and is simply colorblind. This quotes author's complete denial of this and the ignorance the quote purveys is that of pure dominance over the masses.

The government control of markets and the government control of – in this case race – reminds one of Hitler and the control he and his socialist party sought to control – market and race. Ethnic cleansing and free market cleansing has caused countless deaths throughout every government controlled market country throughout history and should not be believed or repeated.

23.

"Advocates of Free Markets are very apt to appeal to the sacred principles of liberty, which are embroiled in one maxim: The fortunate must not be restrained in the exercise of tyranny over the unfortunate."

The free market does allow the fortunate to be unrestrained from success, and as the quote says those without success are unfortunate. Not everyone in the free market is lucky. There are indeed winners and losers, if this feels like tyranny to the less fortunate, it is in no way a crutch, but is more of an inspiration. The free market allows the less fortunate to innovate or in some cases imitate those that are fortunate to find ways towards success. Tyranny can be seen as an evil that something or someone holds over one's head, but free market allows even the unfortunate the ability to leave even the tyranny of those who have been fortunate in one industry to those in that industry, and move to another industry that is more suitable to them and can foster success and fortune.

Liberty does come with it some sense of fear of failure, but its successes are that much more rewarding. After all playing a game that always ends in a stalemate or tie gets very boring and eventually you don't want to play that game anymore and must either invent a new game or learn the rules of a new game to keep the self and the brain stimulated. The free market provides this opportunity of innovation and upward mobility that no other system promises to give.

24.

"You show me a Free Market and I'll show
you a blood sucker."

The bluntness of this quote definitely shows its being and its double speak of ignorance. Of any system, that of socialism creates blood suckers more than the free market. In the free market, one does not have to suck the blood of the unsuspecting as they have choice in their actions (both the employer and employee). Looking to nature we can see the nature of that of a shark in the water. The shark has no neck, no arms and no real way to protect its body from small fish that attach themselves to its side as it swims, it is not built to get rid of these shark clingers. The same with whales, they have large crustaceans that attach themselves and have no defenses to remove them. The government is the same way.

The government does not have any ability to get rid of all the waste and corruption both inside and outside of its organization. Workers (bureaucrats) leech off the government because they have no fear of losing their job. The government makes a budget once a year for the entire fiscal year, the allotted money must be spent and the government employees know this, therefore work less efficiently. In the case of welfare or redistributive payments, people and organizations receiving payments are also leeches and have little to no fear of losing their benefits and take for granted they will be there throughout the fiscal year and for years to come.

These same securities are not normally available in the free market as capital must constantly be created. If there is no payment from the consumer at the end of the month the producer will stop producing or providing goods and services and take their business elsewhere. This ends any attempt at free market producers and consumers from being blood sucking leeches to any one person, place or organization.

25.

"Free Markets are against the things that we say we believe in – Democracy, freedom of choice, fairness. It's not about any of those things now. It's about protecting the wealthy and legalizing greed."

This quote is a good example of how certain words have been demonized and distorted. In all ways free markets promote Democracy, freedom of choice and fairness. In Democracy what do we have? Freedom to choose (to an extent). A free market of political choices, without Democracy how else would we get free markets to buy and sell what we choose. Freedom of choice is exactly what the free market is, nothing else. Lastly fairness, free markets cannot be less fair than say a baseball game or a football game, there is a winner and a loser and as long as you know the rules everyone participates and the skillful succeed.

Looking directly at this quote we can only see some kind of bait and switch that only a used car salesman can pull off and one that has been perpetuated for a long time through propaganda and miseducation about free markets.

26.

"Both climate change and extinction are results of our tyranny over the nonhuman world and our domination of, and exploitation of, whole categories of each other – and those, in turn, are clearly linked to agriculture, the cattle-industrial complex, Free Markets."

According to the author of this quote, freedom is destructive. Allowing people free choice in what and how they consume and produce has devastated the planet. One can assume that the author of this quote therefore has one answer to this devastation, government controlled markets.

If we believe what the author says free markets have exploited whole categories of products which this person links to agriculture and cattle production.

For a counter example let's look at cattle production in China. According to the Straits Times (2016) the cattle production in China has created so much manure they cannot dispose of it. On top of the useless mound of manure there is a lot of ozone depleting methane being produced by the cows and the manure as it sits there rotting.

When government gets involved in an industry, there is waste and lots of it, as in the case with Chinese cattle. Government has no idea how to raise cattle and has destroyed the country in the process, if anything is indeed a destructive force it is government controlled markets.

27.

"Unemployment is the Free Markets way of
telling you to plant a garden."

The free market is such that if you have the ability to grow, you can. The quote uses a garden, plant crops sell them at the market, make money.

In the case of anyone else, use your free time to better yourself, make yourself marketable, and make yourself presentable through cultivation of yourself and your surroundings. Freedom allows this, freedom allows for innovation and the free market will ingest anything that is well cultivated, presentable and better than before.

Chapter IV. Authors of the Quotes

Authors of the quotes in order of appearance (All quotes were retrieved using the website brainyquote.com). In this section authors of the quotes are given a small introduction and all information for each author was taken from various websites listed in parenthesis next to the introduction.

Chapter I. Socialism Quotes

1. "*All Socialism involves slavery*." Herbert Spencer - He was an English sociologist / philosopher, early advocate of the theory of evolution, who achieved an influential amount of knowledge, advocating the preeminence of the individual over society and of science over religion. His best work was The Synthetic Philosophy written in 1896, containing volumes on the principles of biology, psychology, morality, and sociology. (brittanica.com)

2. *"Like the Phoenix, Socialism is reborn from every pile of ashes left day in, day out, by burnt-out human dreams and charred hopes."* Zygmunt Bauman –A writer who examined broad changes in the nature of contemporary society and their effects and individuals and in numerous works that made him one of the most-influential intellectuals in Europe. His most-celebrated books include Modernity and the Holocaust written in 1989, in which he argued that modern industrial and bureaucratic paradigms made the Holocaust imaginable and that the machinery of industrialism also made it possible to carry out, and in Liquid Modernity written in 2000, examined the effects of consumption-based economies, the disappearance of social institutions, and the rise of globalization. (brittanica.com)

3. *"In fact, what were called Socialist countries in Eastern Europe were the most anti-Socialist systems in the world. Workers had more rights in the United States and England than they had in Russia, and it was somehow still called a Government Controlled Market."* Noam Chomsky – An American linguist

whose work from the 1950's revolutionized this field by treating language as a uniquely human, biologically based cognitive capacity. Through his contributions to linguistics and other fields of interest, including cognitive psychology and the philosophies of mind and language, Chomsky has helped to initiate and sustain what has become to be known as the cognitive revolution. Chomsky is known worldwide as a political dissident due to his opinions on the influence of economic elites in U.S. domestic politics, foreign policy, and intellectual culture. (brittanica.com)

4. *"Democracy and socialism have nothing in common but one word: equality. But notice the difference: while democracy seeks equality in liberty, socialism seeks equality in restraint and servitude."* Alexis Detoqueville – Was a political scientist, historian, and politician, best known for Democracy in America written in 1835, a perceptive analysis of the political and social systems of the United States in the early 19th century. (brittanica.com)

5. *"Yes in socialism the rich will be poorer – but the poor will also be poorer. People will lose interest in*

working hard and creating new jobs." Thomas Peterffy – Is a digital trading pioneer. Peterffy is the CEO of Interactive Brokers, which markets its specialized trading platform to sophisticated investors. (forbes.com)

6. *"Compassion is not weakness, and concern for the unfortunate is not socialism."* Hubert H. Humphrey – Was the 38th vice president of the United States from 1965–69 during the Democratic administration of President Lyndon B. Johnson and also the presidential candidate of the Democratic Party in 1968. (brittanica.com)

7. *"Socialism is the ideal state, but it cannot be achieved while man is so selfish."* Annie Besant – Was an Indian independence leader, Fabian socialist, theosophist, and British social reformer. (brittanica.com)

8. *"Socialism is a philosophy of failure, the creed of ignorance, and the gospel of envy, its inherent virtue is the equal sharing of misery."* Winston Churchill - A British statesman, orator, and author who as prime minister from 1940 to 45 and 1951 to 55. He rallied the

British people during World War II and led his country from the brink of defeat to victory. (brittanica.com)

9. *"The problem with socialism is that you eventually run out of other peoples' money."* Margaret Thatcher – Was a British Conservative Party politician and prime minister from 1979 to 1990 and was Europe's first female prime minister. (brittanica.com)

10. *"Socialism in general has a record of failure so blatant that only an intellectual could ignore or evade it."* Thomas Sowell - Dr. Sowell teaches economics at Cornell University and has taught at UCLA as well being a senior fellow at the Hoover Institution in Stanford University since 1980. (breitbart.com)

Chapter II. Government Controlled Markets and Capitalism quotes

11. *"We all too often have socialism for the rich and rugged free market capitalism for the poor."* Martin Luther King Jr. – A Baptist minister and social activist who led the civil rights movement in the United States from the 1950s until his death in 1968. (brittanica.com)

12. *"I am convinced that the path to a new, better and possible world is not capitalism, the path is socialism."* Hugo Chavez – A Venezuelan politician who was president of Venezuela from 1999 to 2013. (brittanica.com)

13. *"They talk about the failure of socialism but where is the success of capitalism in Africa, Asia and Latin America?"* Fidel Castro – The political leader of Cuba from 1959 to 2008. (brittanica.com)

14. *"With the development of industrial capitalism, a new and unanticipated system of injustice, it is libertarian socialism that has preserved and extended*

the radical humanist message of the Enlightenment and the classical liberal ideals that were perverted into an ideology to sustain the emerging social order." Noam Chomsky - See number 3 above.

15. *"During the New Deal, people thought to be liberal was to reject socialism on one extreme and fascism on the other, and to preserve capitalism through regulation and a social safety net."* Noah Feldman - Noah Feldman is Felix Frankfurter Professor of Law at Harvard Law School who specializes in constitutional studies, his particular emphasis is on constitutional design, the relationship between law and religion, and the history of legal theory. (Harvard.edu)

16. *"While there's capitalism, there'll be socialism, because there is always a response to injustice."* Ed Miliband – Mr. Miliband was a Holocaust survivor during World War 2 and is the son of Jewish (and Marxist) refugees. (brittanica.com)

17. *"Feminism is a socialist, anti-family, political movement that encourages women to leave their husbands, kill their children, practice witchcraft, destroy*

capitalism and become lesbians." Pat Robertson – A religious leader, broadcaster, philanthropist, Businessman, educator, and author. He is the founder and chairman of (CBN) The Christian Broadcasting Network Inc. (patrobertson.com)

18. *"I was not chosen to be president to restore capitalism to Cuba. I was elected to defend, maintain and continue to perfect socialism, not destroy it."* Raul Castro – Was a revolutionary who played a pivotal role in the July 26th Movement, which had brought his brother Fidel Castro to power in 1959. He was the defense minister of Cuba from 1959 to 2006 until he became the head of state of Cuba as acting president from 2006 to 08 and president 2008 to 18. (brittanica.com)

19. *"I was guilty of judging capitalism by its operations and socialism by its hopes and aspirations; capitalism by its works and socialism by its literature."* Sidney Hook – An American educator and social philosopher who studied historical theory in its relation to distinctly American philosophy. (brittanica.com)

III. Capitalism Quotes

20. *"Capitalism is the extraordinary belief that the nastiest of men for the nastiest of motives will somehow work together for the benefit of all."* John Maynard Keynes – Was an English economist, best known for his economic theory called Keynesian economics which attempted to understand the causes of long-term unemployment. (brittanica.com)

21. *"There is a contradiction between market liberalism and political liberalism. The market liberals (e.g., social conservatives) of today want family values, less government, and maintain the traditions of society (at least in America's case). However, we must face the cultural contradiction of capitalism: the progress of capitalism, which necessitates a consumer culture, undermines the values which render capitalism possible"* Slavoj Zizek – A Slovene philosopher and cultural theorist whose works address themes in politics, popular culture and psychoanalysis. (brittanica.com)

22. *"We have two evils to fight, capitalism and racism. We must destroy both racism and capitalism."* Huey Newton – An American political activist and cofounder of the Black Nationalist Black Panther Party in the United States.

23. *"Advocates of capitalism are very apt to appeal to the sacred principles of liberty, which are embodied in one maxim: The fortunate must not be restrained in the exercise of tyranny over the unfortunate."* Bertrand Russell – A British philosopher and founding figure of the analytic movement in Anglo-American philosophy. He was the recipient of the Nobel Prize for Literature in 1950. (brittanica.com)

24. *"You show me a capitalist, and I'll show you a bloodsucker"* Malcolm X – An Islamic convert who became a prominent prominent figure in the Nation of Islam in the United States of which he used to articulated concepts of Black Nationalism in the early 1960s. (brittanica.com)

25. *"Capitalism is against the things that we say we believe in - democracy, freedom of choice, fairness. It's not about any of those things now. It's about protecting*

the wealthy and legalizing greed." Michael Moore – An American documentarian filmmaker who is best known for a series of controversial documentaries that address major political and social issues in the United States. (brittanica.com)

26. *"Both climate change and extinction are results of our tyranny over the nonhuman world and our domination of, and exploitation of, whole categories of each other - and those, in turn, are clearly linked to agriculture, the cattle-industrial complex, capitalism."* Lydia Millet – An American conservationist and novelist. (lydiamillet.net)

27. *"Unemployment is capitalism's way of getting you to plant a garden."* Orson Scott Card - Author of the novels Ender's Game, Ender's Shadow and Speaker for the Dead which are widely read by young readers and adults, which are increasingly used in schools. (hatrack.com)

References

Delsol, J., Lecaussin, N. & Martin, E. (2016). *Anti-Piketty: Capital for the 21st Century.* Cato Institute. Washington D.C.

Kornai, J. (1992). *The socialist system: The political economy of communism.* Clarendon Press. Oxford.

Lebowitz, M. (2010). *The socialist alternative: Real human development.* Monthly Review Press. New York.

Steiger, I. & Huang, Z. (2017). "South Korea's new president will have an astronomical level of household debt to deal with." *Quartz.* As seen at https://qz.com/943466/south-koreas-new-president-will-have-an-astronomical-level-of-household-debt-to-deal-with/

Straights Times (2016). "China's giant cow farms polluting the environment with manure and waste." *The Straights Times.* As seen at https://www.straitstimes.com/asia/east-asia/chinas-giant-cow-farms-polluting-the-environment-with-manure-and-waste

Thompson, J. (2003). *Organizations in action: Social science basis of administrative theory.* Transaction Publishers. New Jersey.

Wallerstein, I. (2004). *World-systems analysis: An introduction.* Duke University Press. Durham.

Williamson, L. (2013). "South Korea's growing credit problem." *BBC News.* As seen at http://www.bbc.com/news/world-asia-24059038

Made in the USA
Monee, IL
07 July 2020